Ice Station

IMPRINT

CONCEPT
British Antarctic Survey
Hugh Broughton Architects
AECOM
Galliford Try

AUTHOR
Ruth Slavid

COORDINATION
Claire Curtice Publicists

EDITING
Bronwen Saunders

PROOFREADING
Lisa Schons

GRAPHIC DESIGN
Oliver Kleinschmidt

LITHOGRAPHY, PRINTING AND BINDING
DZA Druckerei zu Altenburg GmbH, Altenburg

© 2015 Park Books AG, Zurich
© for the texts, with the authors
© for the pictures, see picture credits

Park Books AG
Niederdorfstrasse 54
8001 Zurich
Switzerland

www.park-books.com

ISBN 978-3-906027-66-1

FRONT COVER
Halley summer crew returning for 'smoko',
the traditional mid-morning break which
originates from Scott's expeditions to
Antarctica and which the British have
continued ever since.

INSIDE FRONT COVER
Halley VI with science modules to the left,
the red social module in the centre and
habitat modules to the right.

INSIDE BACK COVER
At the end of the summer season a Basler
DC3, operated by Antarctic Logistics Centre
International, ferries people from Halley to
the Russian base at Novolazarevskaya, which
has a blue ice runway. From there they catch
an Ilyushin 76 for the flight back to the heat
of Cape Town.

Ice Station

THE CREATION OF HALLEY VI   BRITAIN'S PIONEERING ANTARCTIC RESEARCH STATION

Ruth Slavid

PARK BOOKS

Superhuman effort isn't worth a damn
unless it achieves results.

ERNEST SHACKLETON (1874–1922)

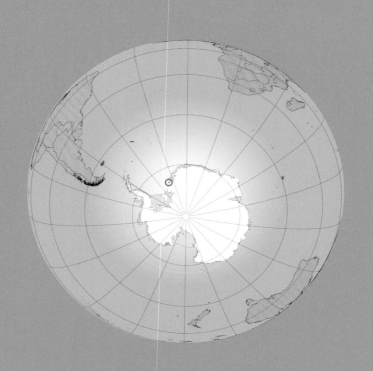

CONTENTS

INTRODUCTION

The Antarctic is the coldest, most remote, and most difficult place in the world to live and work, and the British Antarctic Survey's Halley Research Station is in a particularly difficult part of the continent. It sits on a shifting but featureless ice shelf and is subjected to high winds and annual build-ups of snow that have buried several previous stations. Working there throughout the year involves long months of darkness and, even with modern technology, isolation from family and friends. It is, however, a fantastic place for science, for looking both up above the earth and down into the ice, and for making discoveries that could affect all our futures.

It is because of this that the British Antarctic Survey (BAS) has continued to invest in the difficult and expensive business of sending people there to work. Whether scientists or support staff, these people are not just doing a job but embracing a different way of life. Supporting them so that they can work effectively and enjoy the experience is an essential part of BAS's work. Now it has built a research station that is not only suited to the needs of its staff, but that sets new world standards as a resilient, enduring structure, which is futuristic and arresting from the outside, and welcoming and sustaining on the inside. Designing and building it was an enormous challenge to client, design team and contractor.

This book is a chance to share their story. Very few people will have the opportunity to visit the Halley Research Station, but the photographs in this book give a great impression of what it is like.

RRS James Clark Ross moored at the edge of the Brunt Ice Shelf at the end of the season. Although the ship is primarily used for science research, it also collects members of Halley VI's summer crew to return them to the UK.

CHAPTER 1 # Like nowhere else on Earth

Halley III emerging from the Brunt Ice Shelf
(circa 1992). Approximately 1.2 metres of
snow accumulate each year on the Brunt
Ice Shelf and in the past buildings constructed on the surface became covered and
eventually crushed by snow, necessitating
periodic rebuilding of the station. This part
of the ice shelf is also moving westward by
about 700 metres per year. Halley III was
abandoned in 1984 and this picture was
taken years later when its remains were
spotted emerging from the ice shelf.

Imagine waking up in a comfortable, well-designed, but compact bedroom. Your waking is gentle, because a lamp that simulates daylight has slowly come on. You get up, wash in a communal bathroom, dress and join colleagues for breakfast before starting your working day. This does not sound too difficult to achieve, does it? But imagine that you are working in a place where, while perfectly comfortable indoors, you have to wear special protective clothing if you want to go outdoors. A place that is cut off from the outside world for about eight months of the year, where all your needs have to be delivered by a ship that arrives just twice in the brief summer season, and where the building that you inhabit is not only your home but is all that stands between you and near-certain death.

This is the situation at Halley VI, the newest research station operated by the British Antarctic Survey and the most advanced design built by any nation in the polar regions. As the name suggests, it has had five predecessors. The first was built in 1956 and like its three immediate successors had to be abandoned when buried or crushed by a build-up of snow. This is a particular problem at Halley, where there is snowfall of around 1.2 metres a year. The temperature is very low; in winter it can drop to -50°C, with the lowest ever recorded temperature being -55°C. The snow never melts, therefore, and blown by the prevailing wind it builds up against buildings and other obstacles. The design of Halley V addressed this problem by placing the station on legs that had to be jacked up each year. This was a time-consuming operation, involving all the station's summer staff, who for about two weeks were taken away from their real purpose in being there.

Another problem is the dark. The staff who spend the winter at Halley, when they have no chance to leave, have to cope with 106 days of total darkness. In addition, the station is not actually on the Antarctic continent but on a massive sheet of ice, the Brunt Ice Shelf. This is moving slowly but remorselessly towards the sea. As it approaches and thins, large sections 'calve' or break off as giant icebergs. So even if a station is not buried, its lifespan in any one specific location will be limited.

View from the central module looking into what was described by Herbert Ponting as 'the great white silence'.

Then why work in such a difficult place? The answer is that it is very good for science. It is incredibly expensive to take scientists there and to support them, but the instruments that they use there can discover things in ways that are scarcely possible anywhere else. As Dr. Anna Jones, Senior Tropospheric Chemist with the British Antarctic Survey, explains, 'The most high-profile piece of work done at Halley was the discovery of the hole in the ozone layer in 1985. This was the result of constant monitoring of atmospheric ozone at the station, which began in 1956 and continues to this day. The length of time that the work has taken helps scientists to tell if the hole is actually repairing itself or if this is a natural fluctuation. The US South Pole station also monitors ozone levels, but it misses part of the season because its spring sunrise is later than at Halley.'

Looking at the chemical exchanges that take place between air and snow is also important, and future work will examine emissions of chemicals from the sea ice zone. 'This affects the chemistry in the atmosphere and the number of small aerosol particles, which in turn might affect clouds. Understanding this behaviour will be increasingly important as global warming affects the sea ice. Taking measurements at Halley is ideal,' says Jones, 'because the environment is so simple. There is just ice and ocean.' In contrast, BAS's station Rothera is in a much more complex place, further north on the Antarctic Peninsula and surrounded by mountains and rock.

The other advantage of Halley's position is that it offers 'a window into space weather', as Jones puts it. Satellites orbiting Earth encounter hostile conditions, which are controlled by activity on the Sun – the same activity also triggers the Aurora Australis, the southern aurora, where charged particles hit the Earth's upper atmosphere. Studying the aurora from Halley makes it possible to understand what is happening with space weather, which is a subject of growing importance as it can affect the satellite technology that we use for communications and navigation. Halley's comprehensive suite of scientific instruments provides great insight into what is happening in the region of space close to Earth.

So Halley, despite all its difficulties, is one of the most effective places to carry out science. Supporting the scientists while they are there is central to the design of the latest station, which for the first time in Halley's history offers researchers a home away from home.

Halley I (occupied 1959-1968) was a traditional hut with a pitched roof.

Halley II (occupied 1967-1973) was designed with a pitched roof reinforced with steel supports.

Halley III (occupied 1973-1984) comprised prefabricated huts housed inside corrugated steel conduits.

Halley IV (occupied 1983-1992) was composed of two-storey huts housed inside conduits made from interlocking plywood-faced panels.

Halley V (occupied 1992-2013). To avoid destruction by accumulating snow, the buildings of Halley V were positioned on platforms which were raised every year so that they remained above the ice surface.

A weather balloon is launched every day from Halley. A small package of instruments, called a radiosonde, is attached to the balloon. This measures the temperature, pressure and humidity of the air it passes through and sends the data back to Halley every second. The balloon is tracked throughout its flight using global positioning system (GPS) satellites. The GPS track is converted into information about the wind speed and direction at different heights in the atmosphere.

Communications installations at Halley VI set within the vast emptiness
of the Brunt Ice Shelf.

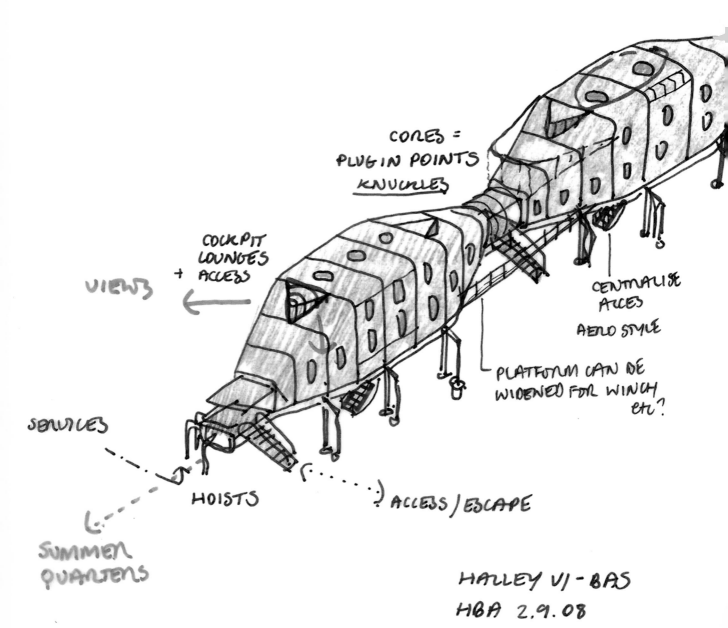

CORES =
PLUG IN POINTS
KNUCKLES

COCKPIT
LOUNGES
+ ACCESS

VIEWS ←

CENTRALISE
ACCES

AERO STYLE

PLATFORM CAN BE
WIDENED FOR WINCH
etc?

ST
LE

SERVICES

HOISTS

? ACCESS / ESCAPE

SUMMER
QUARTERS

HALLEY VI - BAS
HBA 2.9.08

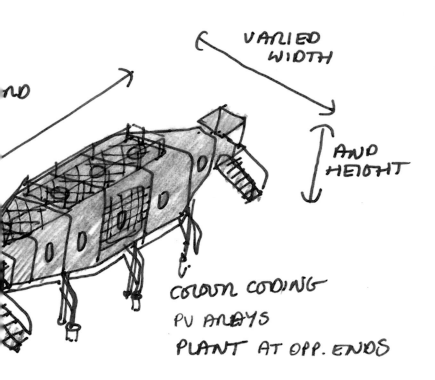

ND

VARIED
WIDTH

AND
HEIGHT

COLOUR CODING
PV ARRAYS
PLANT AT OPP. ENDS

CHAPTER 2

Have skis, will travel

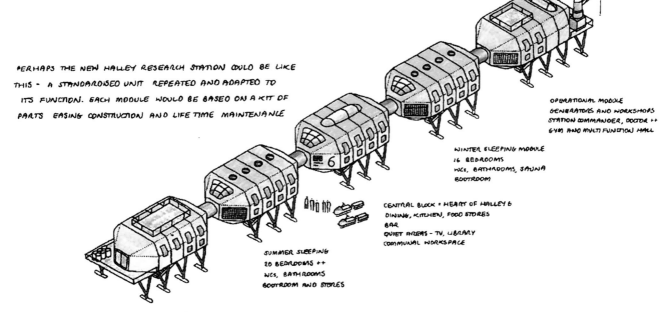

PERHAPS THE NEW HALLEY RESEARCH STATION COULD BE LIKE THIS - A STANDARDISED UNIT REPEATED AND ADAPTED TO ITS FUNCTION. EACH MODULE WOULD BE BASED ON A KIT OF PARTS EASING CONSTRUCTION AND LIFE TIME MAINTENANCE

OPERATIONAL MODULE
GENERATORS AND WORKSHOPS
STATION COMMANDER, DOCTOR ++
GYM AND MULTI FUNCTION HALL

WINTER SLEEPING MODULE
16 BEDROOMS
WCs, BATHROOMS, SAUNA
BOOTROOM

CENTRAL BLOCK = HEART OF HALLEY 6
DINING, KITCHEN, FOOD STORES
BAR
QUIET AREAS - TV, LIBRARY
COMMUNAL WORKSPACE

SUMMER SLEEPING
20 BEDROOMS ++
WCs, BATHROOMS
BOOTROOM AND STORES

SUMMER PLANTROOM
SUMMER KITCHEN AND DINING
WINTER EMERGENCY BACK-UP
VISITORS' SLEEPING - 16 BERTH?

· UNITS MUST APPEAR AERODYNAMIC
· FLOAT ABOVE THE ICE

SEALED POD

ACCESS

HYDRAULIC LEGS

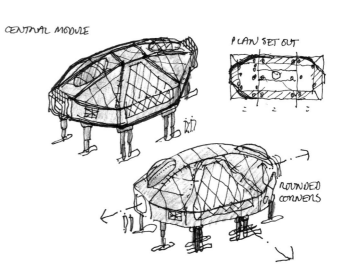

CENTRAL MODULE

PLAN SET OUT

ROUNDED CORNERS

Hugh Broughton's concept sketches, prepared at the start of the design competition, show modules arranged in a line perpendicular to the prevailing wind. Although of similar shape and size, modules are used for different activities. The modules are raised up on hydraulic legs and supported on giant skis to allow for relocation to prevent the base disappearing when a section of the ice shelf breaks away. Early concepts investigated both single- and two-storey modules. The final scheme settled on a single-storey design for the standard modules with a special two-storey central module acting as the social focus of the research station.

When the British Antarctic Survey launched an open architectural competition for a new station at Halley in 2004, it was making a bold move. Because of the technical and logistical difficulties of working there, Britain, like other nations, had tended to focus on solving the engineering challenges while making sure that basic human needs were met – creating what Peter Ayres of AECOM describes as 'an oil platform on ice'.

Karl Tuplin, a civil engineer whom BAS brought in to run the project, explains the thinking behind the competition as follows: 'BAS didn't know what it wanted in terms of a building. It wanted to go to the industry to see what it could do.' It knew it wanted a proposal that would solve some specific problems, in particular the anticipated calving of the ice shelf. This meant that if the station was to last longer than its predecessors (and having stations with an average lifespan of just over a decade is scarcely impressive, if understandable), then it had to be able to move to a new site, ideally more than once. Finding the solution to this problem was one of the main challenges that the design teams had to tackle – along with keeping the station above the snow, working out how to build in the very short summer seasons, and of course keeping everybody warm and dry as well as safe from fire.

Malcolm Reading, whose consultancy specialises in running competitions and who ran the competition for Halley VI together with the Royal Institute of British Architects (RIBA), said, 'This was definitely the most interesting competition that we had ever run.' He helped BAS to write the brief, which included evaluating responses to a questionnaire given to people working and living at Halley V. Reading suggested that, since there were only a handful of architects in the world with experience of designing in the Antarctic (or the Arctic), BAS should widen its criteria. BAS agreed that it was the engineer who should have experience in the region; architects, in contrast, were asked to show ways in which they had worked 'in extreme conditions' of any kind. With the brief written they publicised the call for entries widely, and given the uniqueness of the competition it was picked up by the media and aired on BBC Radio 4, where Hugh Broughton and Michael Wright of AECOM first heard of the competition.

BAS may have been open to new experiences, but it certainly did not expect to end up working with an architect whose practice had never exceeded ten in number, whom few had ever heard of, and whose only completed new building before Halley was a Girl Guides headquarters in South Wimbledon, on the southern edge of London, which cost just over £200,000 to build. That architect was Hugh Broughton, who went along to the briefing for the competition mainly out of curiosity. There he met an old friend, Michael Wright, who at the time was working for the engineering firm Faber Maunsell, now

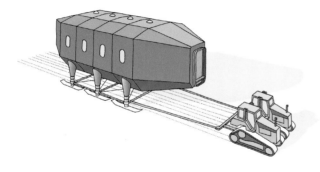

Competition drawing showing the approach to relocation. Modules would be lowered using the hydraulics and towed on the skis using vehicles retained by the British Antarctic Survey in Antarctica.

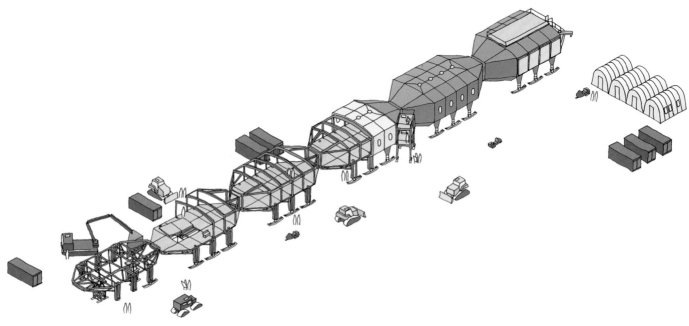

Isometric view showing the proposed factory-line approach to construction.

Concept design for a typical bedroom. The brief stipulated that the rooms should accommodate two people during the summer (for a summer crew of 52) and one person in the winter (for a winter crew of 16). Hugh Broughton's team ensured that the interior would provide a stimulating, psychologically support- ive 'home from home' for the crew.

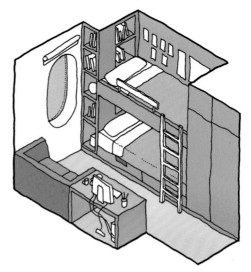

AECOM. The two were filled with enthusiasm for the project, and Wright went back to talk to Peter Ayres, then head of the structural division, about the possibility of taking part in the competition. 'I met Hugh,' Ayres recalls, 'and within five minutes I knew I wanted to work with him.' He was impressed that Broughton was already forming ideas for Halley, as well as by the fact that they had both grown up in the 1960s watching Thunderbirds.

Ayres discovered that some AECOM staff in the US had worked on American Antarctic stations at the South Pole and McMurdo Station, Ross Island. 'We brought them over for a crash course in polar design', he says. Their advice was invaluable since, while the architectural and engineering teams were full of ideas, these more experienced engineers had practical understanding of what might and might not work.

The solution the team came up with envisaged a modular building consisting of several independent but linked units, mounted on skis for transport to new locations. While many elements of the design had to be refined, the fundamental concept was in place from the start. It earned the team a place on the longlist of six bidders, which following inter-views was whittled down to three: the AECOM/Broughton team, a collaboration between BuroHappold Engineering and the architects Lifschutz Davidson Sandilands, and a third bidder made up of Hopkins Architects and Expedition Engineering.

A representative of each team was taken to the Antarctic to learn more from the existing Halley station and refine their submission. Michael Wright was the representative of his team and while there he started looking at the feasibility of using skis that would both act as a foundation and facilitate the relocation of the station.

For Hugh Broughton the most important aspect of the work both before and after winning the competition (he did not visit the site of the station until after they had won) was investigating how people lived in the Antarctic, and what could be done to improve their living conditions. 'We wanted to make it a place to sustain people,' he says, adding, 'I like to think our building does that more than any other.' His endeavours were recognised by Karl Tuplin: 'What Hugh did more than anyone was to look at what we do from the moment the ship arrives. He designed the building around what we actually do.'

The team won the competition, and then the hard work began, which in this case meant detailing the design of a building that could not only operate and be moved in the extraordinary conditions of the Antarctic, but that could also be built there.

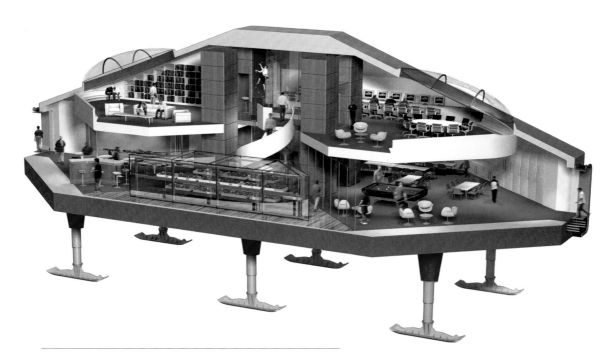

Computer-generated image produced at the final stage of the design competition to demonstrate the flexibility and quality of the interior of the social module. At this stage the design scheme included a hydroponic greenhouse for growing salads and a climbing wall for members of the crew to reach the upper level, a feature which eventually fell victim to a health and safety review when the proximity of the bar was taken into account.

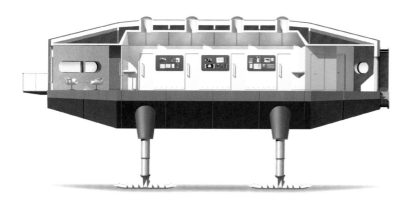

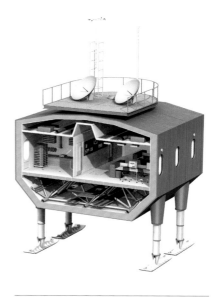

Cross-sectional view of a typical bedroom module. Hugh Broughton Architects worked closely with a colour psychologist, Colour Affects, to develop a special palette for the station. Each module was designed as a destination in its own right. The corridor widens out, the height is increased and natural light is introduced through rooflights to create a bright spacious focal point. The threshold to modules is marked by areas of strong colour and views out to the surrounding landscape, reinforcing the identity of each module and ensuring that the crew feel constantly connected to the Antarctic landscape.

Section through a science module. All the structure is placed around the perimeter to allow flexibility for changes in the scientific programmes inside. The space frame provides a warm zone for service distribution.

View of the northernmost bedroom module, which includes a quiet lounge for smaller groups who want to take time out from the main community.

Computer-generated image produced at the final stage of the competition when the design included 12 modules rather than the eight that were eventually constructed.

CHAPTER 3 # First things first

Computer-generated image produced during
the detail design stage. This image bears an
extraordinary likeness to the final building.

The design of Halley VI became iconic long before it was complete, being used widely on BAS's publicity material and even appearing on stamps. At that stage the images were all computer-generated, although the final result was remarkably similar, even if at one point in the design process three modules were removed owing to the need to cut costs.

The largest central module is the main social space, which is distinguished not only by its size but also by the fact that it is bright red, whereas all the others are blue. These other modules (including an observatory) are used either for working or for sleeping. The well-appointed, while compact bedrooms, are intended for single occupancy in winter but are occupied by two people in summer. Some of the summer visitors sleep in an older existing annex building which has been retained.

Modular buildings seemed an obvious solution, not only to the challenge of relocating the station, but also to the construction process itself. With a summer season lasting a maximum of 12 weeks, construction time was bound to be limited even when spread over a number of years; so prefabricating as much as possible off site was desirable. 'The fundamental decision to make it modular was to do with logistics', says Peter Ayres. Ships unload onto the sea ice and then elements have to be towed on a sledge. The maximum weight allowed is 9.5 tonnes, of which 3.5 tonnes is the weight of the sledge. The designers wanted to prefabricate the largest elements possible to cut down on construction time. By putting the frames on skis, they eliminated the weight of the sledge and were left only with determining how large a steel frame they could prefabricate within the given weight limit.

The other main area of design development concerned the details of the skis attached to the modules and the mechanism for lifting and lowering them. When Hugh Broughton and Peter Ayres first went to Antarctica after winning the competition, Ayres spent the time carrying out experiments with bulldozers to determine how large a weight it was possible to tow in the snow. 'We were told you can never move more than 20 tonnes in Antarctica', he explains. 'In fact we have moved more than 200 tonnes.' He worked on this with Peter Willmott, contract manager for the contractor Galliford Try. Unlike AECOM, which had experience of the Antarctic only in another part of the business, and Broughton, who had no such experience, Galliford Try had previously – in fact only recently – worked for BAS in the Antarctic. They therefore understood the logistical and other challenges of working there.

Vehicle testing being conducted at Halley V in 2006, during a site visit by Hugh Broughton, Peter Ayres and Peter Willmott. A test sledge loaded with vehicles to simulate the weight of a module was successfully pulled by two bulldozers, proving that the proposed relocation strategy could work.

Hugh Broughton and Peter Ayres during a research trip to Halley V. One Twin Otter plane remains at Halley in the summer to help establish and monitor remote science installations.

In 2006 the design team visited Halley V, flying via the Falkland Islands and the British Antarctic Research Station at Rothera. The journey took two weeks to allow for specialist training and bad weather. In the final leg the team flew in a Twin Otter from Rothera Station and were seen off by two Adélie penguins.

The team developed skis that were very robust and able to lock in place or rotate independently. Having originally intended to raise the modules above the snow accumulation with airbags, the design team changed to hydraulics. This meant that the legs had to be changed from splayed to vertical, an idea that Ayres sold to Broughton by telling him that it made the station look more like Thunderbird 2.

The space-age connotations drop away, however, when it comes to the interior. 'I really wanted people to feel at home', Broughton says. The double-height space in the central red module can be used in a number of different ways and is thus a flexible space in a location where so much else is constrained. 'It is the only double-height space in the Antarctic', says Broughton. The team went through a lot of what he considers traditional architectural moves, in other words thinking about how people would interact with space. Thus, at the end of each module the corridor widens in front of the bathroom to facilitate informal interactions as people pass. Each desk contains a flip-up mirror so that people can check how they look before joining their colleagues. Floors are carpeted, as the most comfortable finish, and Broughton worked with a colour consultant to ensure that the decor would encourage feelings of calm and comfort. At the same time he felt it was vital to have views of the surroundings and of the sky, as well as a brief outdoor trudge between the two sides of the station, so that people would not become too comfortable and forget where they are.

Broughton describes the design as 'a high-tech building in a great British tradition; a building designed for the future which is based on first principles.'

ROOF LEVEL

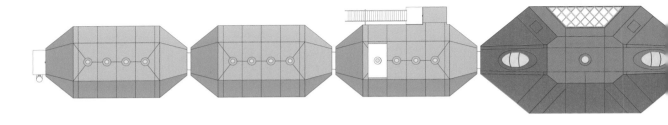

UPPER LEVEL

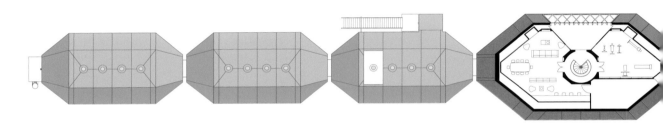

OPERATIONAL LEVEL

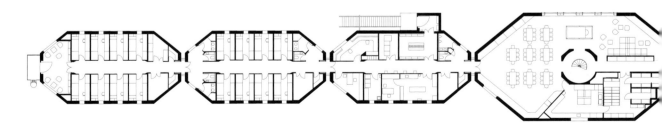

Module B2 Sleeping Module	**Module B1** Sleeping Module	**Module C** Command Module	**Module A** The Robert Falcon Scott Module

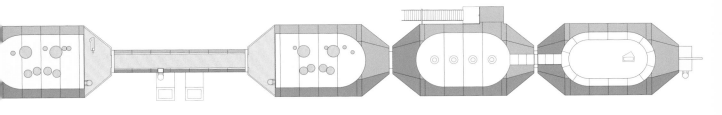

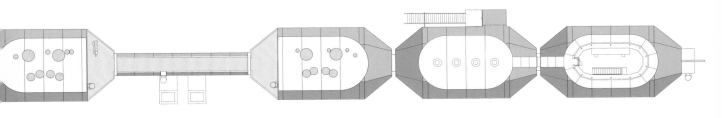

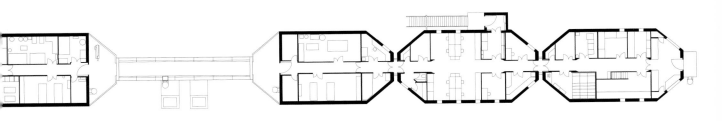

Module E 1	Service Link	Module E 2	Module H 1	Module H 2
Generators and Plant		Generators and Plant	Science Module	Science Module

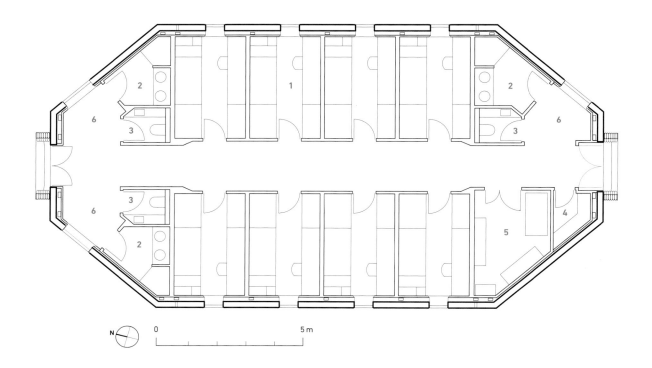

Bedroom module Plan

1 Bedroom
2 Shower room
3 WC
4 Toiletries store
5 Plant room
6 Threshold space

N

0   5 m

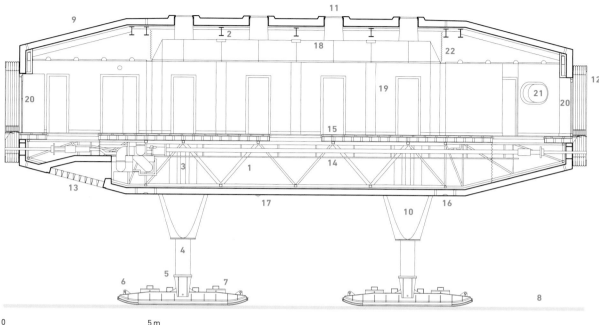

0   5 m

Bedroom module Section

1 Intumescent coated-steel space frame substructure

2 Intumescent coated-steel superstructure arranged around perimeter to maximise internal flexibility

3 Hydraulically operated cassette within paired steel rectangular hollow section (RHS) structure

4 Steel circular hollow section (CHS) leg wrapped in high-performance insulation and mandrel wrapped with GRP skin

5 Solid EPDM thermal break between ski and leg

6 Lehmann steel skis used as spreader foundations and for relocation

7 Steel 'centre boards' lock modules to the ice under severe wind load

8 Ice surface

9 Glass reinforced polymer (GRP) cladding incorporating polyisocyanurate (PIR) closed-cell foam insulation with overall U-value of 0.113 Wm²K

10 Insulated GRP thigh cladding to bracing at leg connection to space frame

11 Triple-glazed rooflights with 27% light transmission factor and U-value of 1 Wm²K, structurally glazed into GRP panels

12 Insulated double-skin flexible-silicone rubber connectors allow for differential settlement between modules

13 Pultruded GRP grille to air intake and extract protects inner aluminium diffuser grilles from spindrift (small particles of windborne ice)

14 Prefabricated service cassette within space frame void

15 Prefabricated steel-and-timber floor cassettes with integrated paired Surespan access panels for maintenance access, finished with carpet in bedroom modules and studded rubber in working modules

16 Jacking point for temporary hydraulic jacking tower, used to prop modules during annual lifting process

17 Warning beacon flashes when module is being lifted with the hydraulics

18 Phenolic GRP internal ceiling linings with integral access panels and light tubes to rooflights

19 Painted glass-fibre-faced Fermacell wall linings with integral movement joints and rebated painted skirtings

20 Steel-framed glazed fire doors between modules

21 Porthole windows with integral black-out blinds provide views out on the ice at regular points along the length of the station

22 Fire barrier

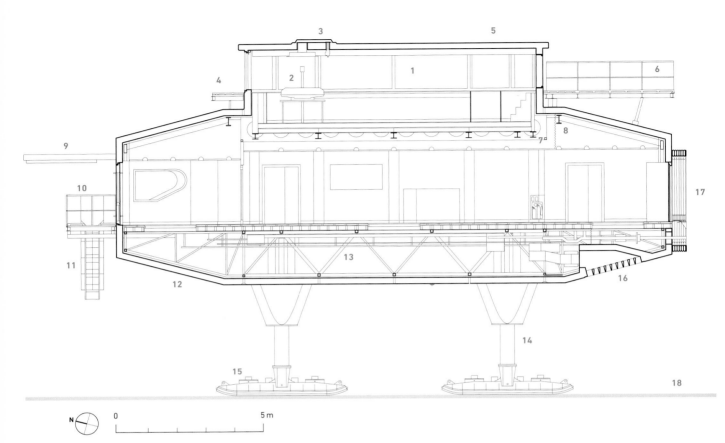

Science module Section

1 Triple glazing fixed to GRP mullions incorporating blinds for winter blackout

2 Dobson spectrophotometer

3 Access hatch with mechanical geared opening allows regular ozone readings

4 Access walkway

5 Insulated GRP structure to meteorological observatory

6 Bridge link to roof deck on neighbouring science module

7 Castellated beam allows service connectivity across module ceiling space

8 Fire barrier

9 GRP encapsulated insulated winch beam for lifting of science equipment to working level

10 Balcony

11 Drop-down galvanised ladder for fire escape

12 Painted GRP cladding incorporating PIR closed-cell foam insulation

13 Intumescent coated steel space frame substructure

14 Hydraulic operated GRP encapsulated insulated steel leg

15 Steel skis used as spreader foundation and for relocation

16 Pultruded GRP grille to air intake and extract protects inner aluminium grilles from spindrift (small particles of windborne ice)

17 Insulated double skin flexible connectors between modules

18 Ice surface

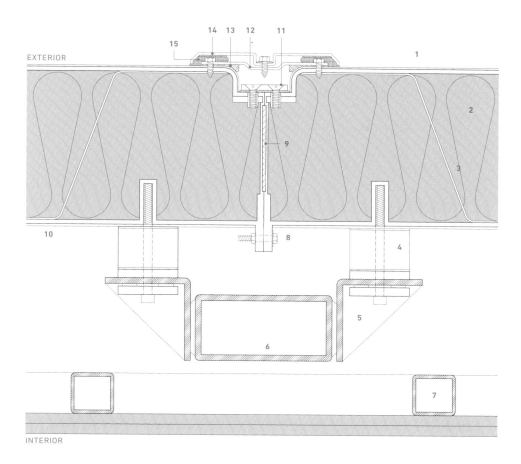

EXTERIOR

INTERIOR

Cladding detail

1 GRP outer skin to panels finished with gel coat and oversprayed with polyurethane acrylic automotive paint to ensure UV stability. Filled polyester resin used to achieve 30-minute fire resistance

2 190 mm polyisocyanurate (PIR) closed-cell foam insulation to achieve U-value of 0.113 Wm²K

3 Resin-infused cross-fibres prevent delamination under wind load

4 Flexible elastic-silicone cladding mounting screwed into GRP 'hard points' cast into panels

5 Steel cladding brackets welded to primary steel superstructure

6 Steel superstructure finished in intumescent coating to achieve one-hour fire resistance. Steel grade selected for performance at extremely low temperatures

7 Steel structure to prefabricated room pods (bedrooms, bathrooms, offices, etc). Pods lined in Fermacell board selected for rigidity and acoustic performance

8 Panels bolted together through GRP flanges using stainless-steel fixings

9 Continuous compressible neoprene insulation maintains thermal performance at joints, finished with PTFE to reduce friction during installation

10 GRP inner skin to panels finished with intumescent paint to achieve Cs3d2 (Class 0) surface spread of flame characteristics

11 Panels jointed with GRP jointing strip fixed with countersunk M10 stainless-steel cap screws through compressed foam neoprene gasket

12 Extruded aluminium internal cover mounting strip

13 Aluminium mounting strip fixed with coach screws. Foamed EPDM compressed gasket seal between mounting strip and panel.

14 Extruded aluminium external cover strip finished with polyurethane acrylic automotive paint to match panel finish, fixed to internal aluminium mounting strip with self-drilling stainless-steel fasteners

15 Junction cover gasket formed in foamed EPDM

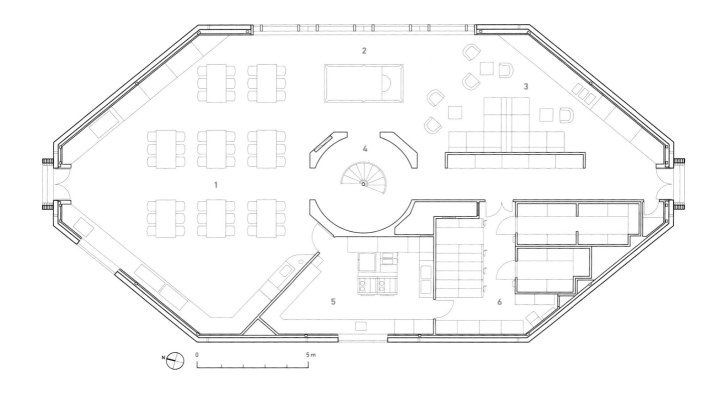

Social module Main plan

1 Dining area
2 Games area in double height space
3 Bar area
4 Stairs to upper level
5 Kitchen
6 Food stores

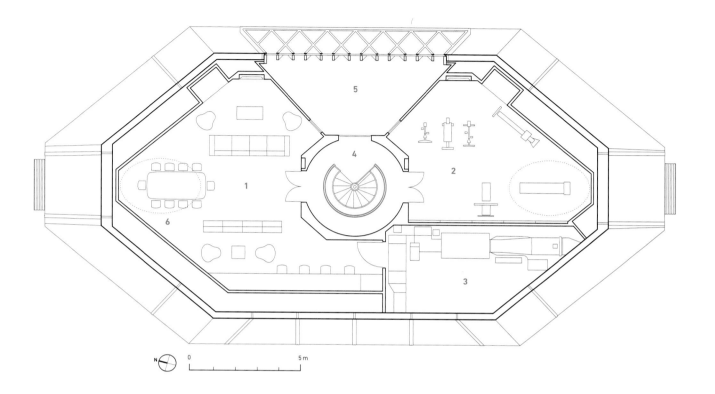

Social module Upper plan

1 TV lounge and meeting room
2 Gym
3 Plant room
4 Stair
5 Double height space
6 Outline of cockpit rooflight

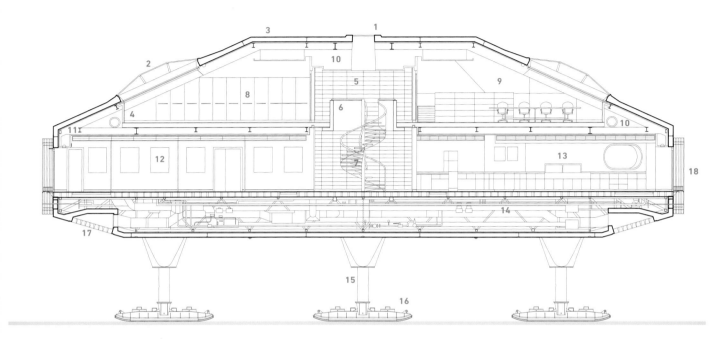

N

0   5 m

Social module Section

1 Triple glazed rooflight centred over spiral stair

2 Double glazed curved oval cockpit rooflight allows full views of auroral displays in winter

3 Painted GRP cladding incorporating PIR closed-cell foam insulation with overall U-value of 0.113W/m²k

4 Painted glass fibre faced Fermacell wall linings with integral movement joints

5 Lebanese cedar veneered curved wall panels to stair hub

6 Solid balustrade to upper landing of spiral stair

7 Satin stainless steel, cherry and glass spiral stair

8 Gym

9 TV lounge and meeting room

10 Service distribution to upper level

11 Intumescent coated steel superstructure

12 Bar lounge with historic photos mounted on wall

13 Servery

14 Service distribution to lower level within space frame substructure

15 Hydraulically operated CHS leg wrapped in high performance insulation and mandrel wrapped with GRP skin

16 Steel skis

17 Pultruded GRP grille to air intake and extract

18 Insulated double skin flexible silicone rubber connectors between modules

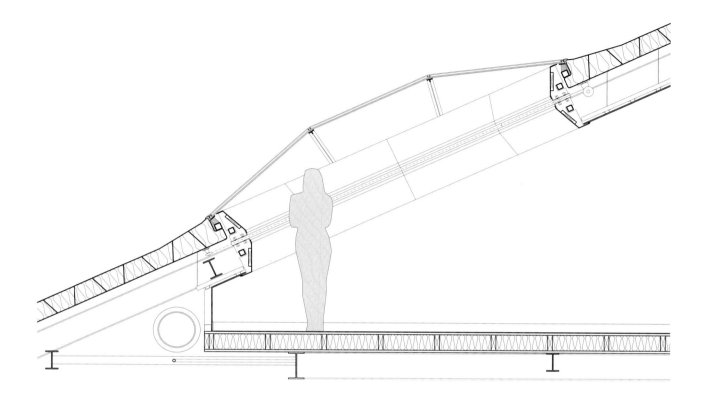

Social module Cockpit rooflight detail

Two special cockpit rooflights allow residents to observe the spectacular
auroral light displays, which take place in the winter months in the skies
above Halley, from the warmth of the upper decks of the main social module.
The double-glazed units were curved in Italy, fabricated in the Netherlands
and installed into the cladding in South Africa – demonstrating the global
scope of the project. Large electric blackout blinds descend down the rooflights.

CHAPTER 4

Extreme team

Towards the end of the third construction
season the modules were moved from Halley V
to the site of Halley VI. The 15 kilometres journey
took one and a half hours. Weighing just over
200 tonnes, the main social module was one of
the largest loads ever moved on ice.

The key to the construction of Halley VI was preparation. As much of the station's structure as possible was prefabricated, largely in the UK and South Africa. Elements were preassembled for testing, and then everything had to be loaded and accounted for, then unloaded on site in such a way to ensure that each item could be located as required.

John Hammerton, International Operations Director of Galliford Try, the main contractor, explains, 'The client has to be very clear about specifying the brief. The designers have to turn it into something buildable. We have to turn what is on the drawings into bits and pieces of material. They have to fit. We spent a lot of time with the designers checking that everything was detailed on the drawings so we could buy it before we got there.'

The working spaces within the units were constricted, which meant that everything had to be brought into them on a just-in-time basis. Elements had to be packaged into small containers, and there was a long supply line, carefully documented on a spreadsheet. (Because the supply line was outside, it was not possible to use barcodes as the scanners would have been confused by frost.) This was a mammoth logistics operation and, as Hammerton says, 'We did not lose one box.'

Without wanting to be extravagant, the contractor took along more spare equipment than is usually needed on a construction site, for instance increasing the amount of extra plasterboard to allow for damage above the usual standard of 7.5 percent. On most sites there is a balance between oversupply and contingency, but this balance shifts when there is no option to pick up some more at the local builder's merchant.

Trial erection of a standard blue module in Cape Town gave the construction crew valuable experience in putting the buildings together and offered a chance to test the hydraulics and the air tightness of the cladding.

At least as important as planning for materials was planning for people. Everybody who was brought to the site had to be housed, fed, clothed, given work to do, kept safe, and even given time off. Returning home safely was given the highest priority. BAS helped with the selection process to ensure that potential employees had the right attitude to work in the Antarctic.

It was incredibly important that the workforce was flexible. Whereas normally a skilled tradesperson would stick to his or her specialisation, here a steel erector, for example, might be required to use his normal skills at the start of the season and then help with decorating at the end. Because of this, and very unusually for a construction site, all members of the construction team were paid the same, regardless of their specialisms.

When AECOM wanted to send out an engineer one season, there was such a shortage of space that they were told they could only send somebody who could double as a worker on the steel team as well – which they did.

The new station was built next to the old station and the elements then towed to their new home, 15 kilometres away, on a specially prepared ice road. The main difficulty in towing was overcoming 'stiction', the friction between the skis and the ice. A specially designed element connecting the units to the bulldozers that were pulling them allowed the bulldozers to gain some traction before actually connecting to the loads.

The individual units, once in place, were joined by Trelleborg connectors, the kind of concertina systems that connect carriages on metro trains. This required a large degree of precision, but as one of the last demanding tasks on a project that had never been simple, the construction team not surprisingly succeeded with aplomb.

Erection of the steel frame of a trial module in Cape Town, and testing of the hydraulic leg system.

Trial erection of the main social module was a surreal sight in suburban Cape Town.

The components of construction were delivered to Antarctica in a giant ice-strengthened Russian cargo vessel – the Anderma. Bow and stern lines were moored in the sea ice. Mooring points had to be prepared in advance of the ship's arrival. These entailed excavating 2 metre deep holes into the ice and setting timbers into the excavation with anchor ropes extending to the surface. The holes were refilled with compacted snow which then refroze, providing secure mooring points.

As the sea ice is rarely more than 2-3 metres thick and can be very fragile, the British Antarctic Survey stipulated that the largest load which could be unloaded could not weigh more than 9 tonnes, including the sledge. The station therefore had to be constructed as a series of pre-fabricated components, which could be towed up onto the ice shelf and onto Halley V where they could be fitted together. The largest component was the steel space frame substructure of a standard module. Once on the ice shelf, loads were consolidated for onward transport to the construction site.

STAGE 1 Space frame of a standard module supported on its transit skis, having just arrived at Halley V.

STAGE 2 The module raised on shipping containers to allow hydraulic legs and Lehmann skis to be installed.

STAGE 5 Prefabricated plant installed onto the floors of one of the energy modules. The white boxes are generators.

STAGE 6 Steel superstructure fitted over the prefabricated plant, ready to receive the cladding. The pink boxes are fuel tanks.

STAGE 3 Hydraulic legs and Lehmann skis installed.

STAGE 4 Prefabricated timber floor cassettes being installed onto the space frame, creating both a working platform and the floor of the modules.

STAGE 7 Glass-reinforced plastic pre-glazed cladding panels were lifted into position and fixed to the steel frame. The cladding design maximised the size of the panels to minimise the erection time. The base cones were made from a series of flat panels bonded together in the factory to create complex geometric forms, which could be lifted into position as fast as possible.

STAGE 8 The glazed panels of the atrium being fitted to the red social module.

Installation of one of the giant Lehmann steel skis, which form both the module foundation and the means of relocation.

Checking the seals on a cladding panel prior to the installation of the nose cones.

The station was erected using a factory line approach to construction, which was inspired by a visit to the JCB manufacturing facility in the UK. Crews were dedicated to either the blue modules or the large red social module. The modules were erected at Halley V so that the crew could use the accommodation and facilities provided by British Antarctic Survey.

This photo captures members of the construction crew, known as the 'Extreme Team' enjoying 'smoko' after the daily team briefing. This group of extraordinarily dedicated and skilled people realised the dreams of the clients and the aspirations of the designers in one of the world's most challenging environments.

ence module being pulled from Halley V to Halley VI.

The first modules being joined together at Halley VI.

ection of the bridge link between the two energy
odules at the site of Halley VI.

Spring 2011, the winter crew of Halley V visit the Halley VI site
to check on the condition of the modules.

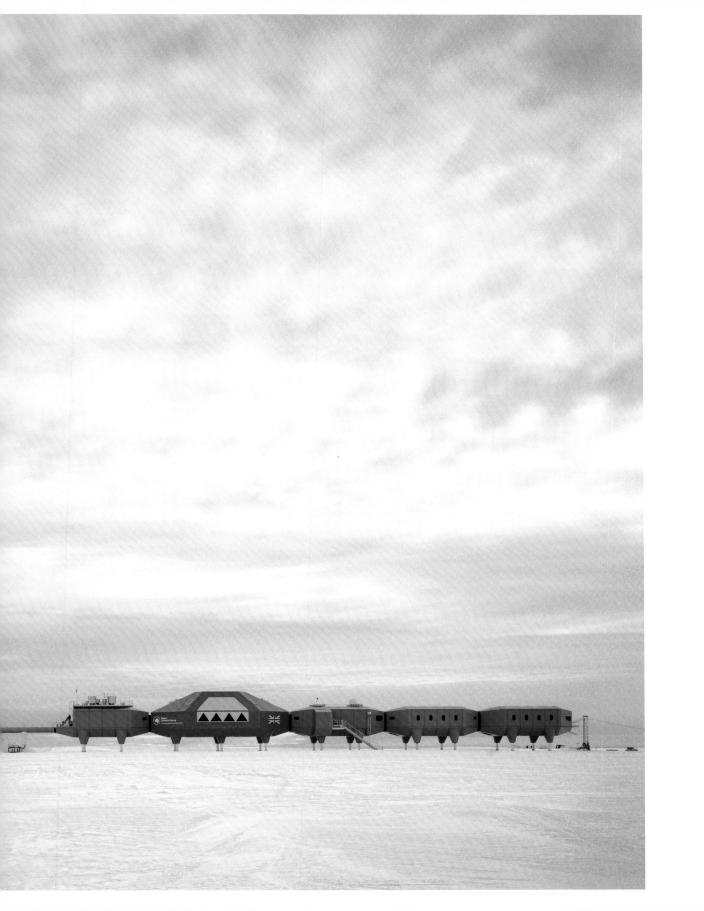

CHAPTER 5

Life in the freezer

Double-height space at the heart of the social module. It is glazed with translucent panels insulated with Nanogel, giving high levels of both thermal insulation and light transmittance. The material was originally developed by the space industry. Clear glazing at the base of the window gives views of the Antarctic wilderness.

Living in the Antarctic is a special and difficult experience, although for the right people also an inspiring one. Summer visitors have an intense time, rushing to complete their specified tasks as well as helping with work such as unloading the supply ship and getting a taste of the Antarctic environment. The overwinterers spend around 14 months in the Antarctic, coping with the isolation, the darkness and the extreme cold. The stations ameliorate the dislocation by imposing rigid work and meal schedules so that people do not lose track of time. There are also special events; Midwinter's Day for example is a time of major celebration.

Isolation is still an issue, but its nature has changed with improved communications. As emailing and telephoning have become easier, the need for senior scientists to be present over winter has lessened, since they can direct their work from BAS's Cambridge headquarters. Halley has a Cambridge telephone number, so calls are 'local'. Although bandwidths are not great enough to allow people to stream television or video, portable technology allows them to watch recorded material in their rooms rather than communally.

These changes have taken place alongside and parallel to the construction of Halley VI. Whereas decades ago the station was occupied by bearded men bent on roughing it and carrying out tasks such as cutting up seal meat to feed the dogs (dogs have long since been banished from the Antarctic), now life is much easier physically; and rightly so. Going to Halley is not an adventure holiday, after all, but a way of furthering scientific research, and the station needs to assist that process in as effective a way as possible.

Bedrooms were prefabricated with all the furniture pre-installed. Each room includes a bunk bed, a desk and plenty of storage. The design team developed a special alarm light, which was installed next to each bed head. This can be used for reading and as an alarm clock, waking residents with daylight simulation equivalent to a false dawn, to help combat seasonal affective disorder, one of the psychological challenges of life in the polar regions.

Nevertheless, life there is not like a luxury hotel. Everybody has to be willing to join in with necessary tasks, including regular cleaning known as 'gash'. All water has to be melted in a melt tank, although the new system involves using a bulldozer rather than hand shovelling. Nobody is allowed to go beyond a perimeter line around the station without prior arrangement for fear of their getting lost, and there are handlines to lead people back to the station in case of a whiteout or on an overcast winter's night. Cooks learn special tricks, such as carefully turning eggs in the refrigerator so that they can last up to 14 months. And most of the men do still grow beards.

Some of the instruments are housed in converted freight containers as much as a kilometre away from the base station to ensure that they are in completely clean air. 'One engineer is responsible for each instrument', explains Mike Pinnock, a board member for science delivery at BAS. 'When things are not going well, there's just you.'

Agnieszka Fryckowska, who has worked as summer and winter Station Leader (previously known as Base Commander) at both Halley V and Halley VI, says, 'Halley VI is quite luxurious compared to Halley V. We have fantastic windows. Last time I was there it was so lovely to look out. By comparison Halley V was like an old-fashioned shoebox. Some of the rooms had no windows.'

When people arrive and see the futuristic-looking station for the first time, they are 'so excited', she says, 'they just want to rush around doing everything'. When Hugh Broughton was lucky enough to visit the new station briefly during the snagging, he saw that people were pulling dining tables through into the double-height space in a way that had not been envisaged. In other words, they were treating it like home. There can be no greater accolade.

The main command module includes the Station Leader's office, doctor's surgery, communications room, principal boot room, server, laundry and a hairdressing cupboard. Rooflights bring natural light into the heart of the module for 24 hours a day during the summer months.

Grab
Bag

Left: Small kitchenette

Right: WC.
The station has a vacuum drainage system, which has helped reduce water usage to just 20 litres per person per day. By comparison at Halley V the crew were using 120 litres per person per day whilst in Europe people use on average 160-180 litres per person per day. Reduced water usage is one of the great environmental successes of the station's design.

The main boot room. The architect developed bespoke designs for all the furniture following detailed conversations with previous Halley residents. The perforated shelves in the boot-room allow warm air to percolate from top to bottom, drying gloves and hats as well as overalls and coats.

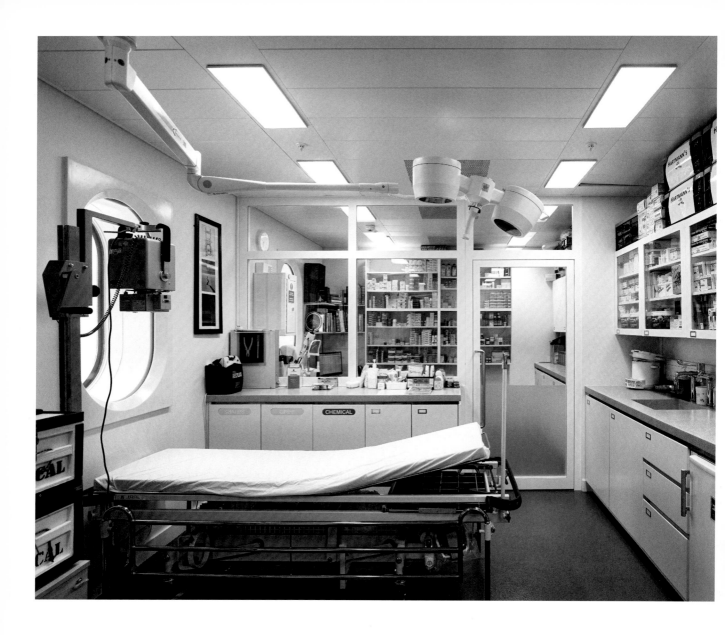

The doctor's surgery includes facilities for surgical operations and basic dentistry.

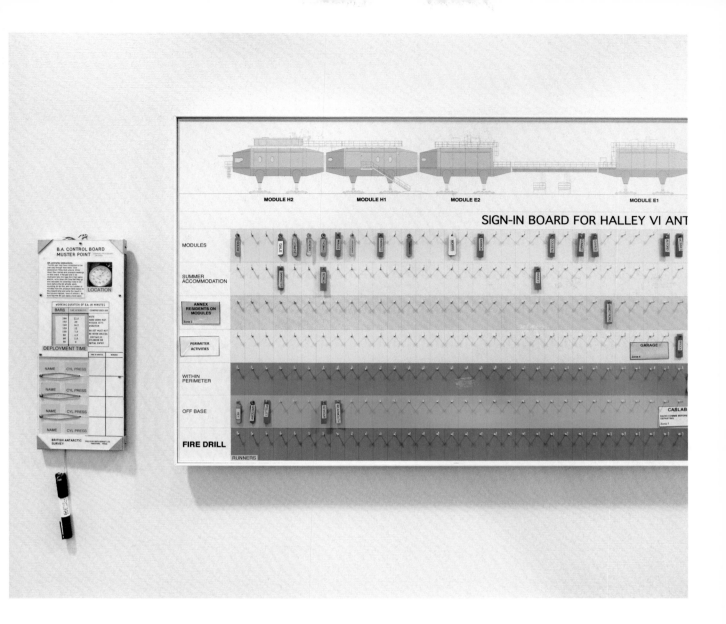

The signing in/out board helps monitor the location of all crew members,
ensuring their safety.

The communications hub includes an air traffic control facility with
direct views through an extra large window to the ski way.

The lower level of the social module provides space for dining, the bar and noisier recreation, whilst the upper level accommodates the gym and the TV lounge.

The flexible, open plan layout of the lower level of the central module encourages social interaction. Dining, games and the bar area are all contained within one free-flowing space arranged around a double height, light-filled atrium. This approach helps to reinforce a strong sense of community.

The drum containing the spiral stair, which leads to the upper level, is lined in Lebanese cedar veneered panels. The veneer was selected for its pleasant scent. The use of smell is a design device to help residents overcome the sensory deprivations of living in the Antarctic desert.

Both the upper level lounge and the gym incorporate 'cockpit' rooflights to allow residents to immerse themselves in the fantastic auroral displays which are common at Halley in winter (without having to endure the outdoor temperatures which can be as low as -55˚C).

Bridge link between the energy modules allows sharing of power, data and
water systems and is also a handy route from the habitat to the science modules.

Halley VI is an entirely self-sufficient infrastructure-free scientific research facility. The station includes twin energy modules for resilience and life safety, which are linked by a bridge. These modules incorporate fuel storage, generators, water treatment plant, fire suppression systems and sewage treatment plant. The sewage is treated in a bioreactor and the resultant sludge is incinerated. Water is produced by melting snow in two semi-buried melt tanks placed under the mid-point of the bridge.

Upper-level climate observatory with 360° views of the Brunt Ice Shelf.

Ozone readings have been taken at Halley since 1957 and continue at Halley VI,
using a Dobson spectrophotometer.

Much of the scientific data is collected at Halley by remote radar and electro-magnetic arrays, which require regular upkeep. Electrical workshops in the science modules provide warm space for technicians to work on components before eventually going out onto the ice to carry out essential repairs and maintenance.

Storms regularly batter the station, with winds sometimes exceeding 150 km/h.
At other times cold mists engulf the Brunt Ice Shelf creating white-out conditions.

Entrance to the science modules. Stairs can be lifted on chains when
the station is relocated. Roof decks provide space for science equipment.

Double-height social module at the heart of the station. The hatches allow
for escape in case of fire using spring-loaded descenders.

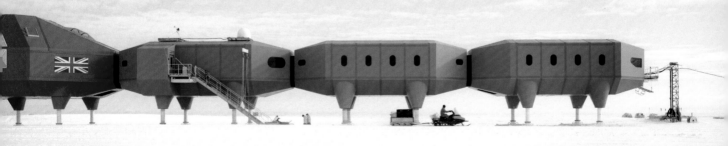

CHAPTER 6   Into the future

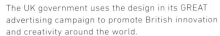

The UK government uses the design in its GREAT advertising campaign to promote British innovation and creativity around the world.

The station design has featured on special stamps issued during the competition, and also on commemorative coins produced by the British Antarctic Territory following its construction.

The ground-breaking design symbolises a future which fuses optimism and technology, and has captured the imagination of architects and artists around the world. It has featured in numerous magazines, on TV and on radio and has been exhibited globally, including the British Council touring exhibition 'Ice Lab: New Architecture and Science in Antarctica' and in the Antarctic Pavilion of the 14th International Architecture Exhibition, La Biennale di Venezia, 2014, the first time the continent has been represented in a Venice Biennale.

Halley VI has gained critical acclaim internationally, winning industry awards and garnering press interest in all four corners of the globe. It is one of few buildings to appear on a coin, and it even prompted the genesis of an Antarctic Pavilion at the Venice Architecture Biennale 2014, all of which will help to secure its place in the canon of architecture.

There is no denying that the Halley VI station is a magnificent achievement, but does its originality make it irrelevant beyond its own boundaries? Not at all. It has changed thinking about building in the Antarctic and other remote places; it has taught all those involved in its construction an enormous amount; and it has ensured that there will be a good environment in which Antarctic science can continue to develop in the future in ways that cannot be foreseen. 'Almost nothing was known about atmospheric chemistry', Anna Jones explains. 'Now we have learned that there is an awful lot going on.' It is only from the results of current work that the direction of future projects will be determined.

The team of Hugh Broughton Architects and AECOM has been appointed to work on other Antarctic stations; it reached the final stage of a competition for the design of the Korean station; it won the appointment and is currently building the Spanish station; and it is also designing a National Science Foundation funded atmospheric watch laboratory in Greenland. Looking even further afield, Broughton was invited to a brainstorming session with NASA scientists to discuss the minimal spatial requirements for people on a 30-month manned mission to Mars. And the station's impact has also spread within the Antarctic itself, with stations such as India's new Bharati station showing far higher design quality than any earlier models.

Halley VI has made technological advances as well, particularly in the way it has used prefabrication so effectively, and increased knowledge about the loads that can be towed on ice.

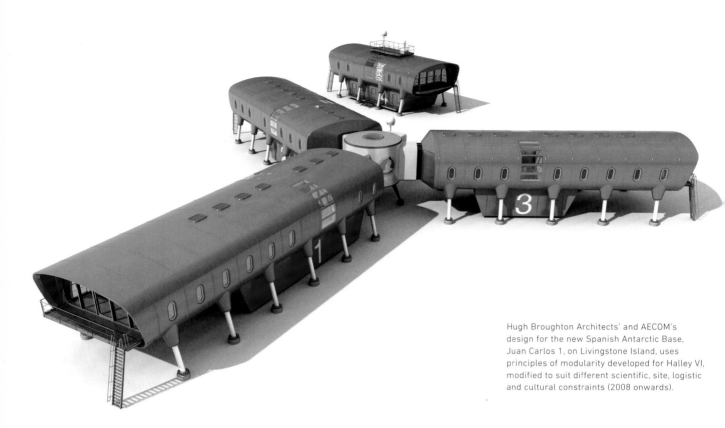

Hugh Broughton Architects' and AECOM's design for the new Spanish Antarctic Base, Juan Carlos 1, on Livingstone Island, uses principles of modularity developed for Halley VI, modified to suit different scientific, site, logistic and cultural constraints (2008 onwards).

Hugh Broughton Architects' and AECOM's design for an Atmospheric Watch Observatory for the US National Science Foundation, to be located at the summit of the Greenland Ice Cap (2012 onwards).

Drawing upon its increasingly extensive experience in cold regions, Hugh Broughton Architects has developed a concept for a relocatable mini-module to support remote science and logistics. The modules would use the cladding as the structure to minimise erection time, and would make maximum use of solar and wind energy to minimise the amount of fuel needed for their operation.

Hugh Broughton Architects collaborated with Samoo and Samsung on the design of a new Korean Antarctic research station on Terra Nova Bay.

Hugh Broughton Architects' designs have signalled the birth of a new movement in Antarctic architecture with other nations now creating similarly futuristic designs, including BOF Architekten's elegant Bharati Station for India in the Larsemann Hills, which was built using 134 specially adapted shipping containers.

But just as Broughton sees the design of the station interior as a development in line with the best traditional architectural thinking, it is the return to some older values that makes the project all the more unusual. Galliford Try recruited and employed its workforce directly, whereas today most projects are carried out by subcontractors. With a scheme of this complexity, where everything had to go right, 'we couldn't have done it with sub-contractors', says John Hammerton. Similarly, for the architect and engineer there had to be a return to a way of working that has too often been lost. Almost everything had to be worked out from first principles, rather than simply building from codes. Every aspect of the building was thought through and was drawn in detail before construction started. 'The type of thinking that I did for Halley VI now defines my approach to all my projects', Broughton says, 'whether I am designing an art gallery or an office'.

This was the biggest project that Broughton had ever done, but for AECOM the size is relatively modest. And yet, Peter Ayres says, 'The impact that it has had on our business has been enormous. It makes people realise that we can do genuine, clever design.' And for the individuals who worked on the station, it has freed their thinking, allowing them to design from first principles on projects such as the cooled stadia for the Qatar World Cup – a climate as different from Halley as one could imagine.

This may not be relevant to the scientists working at Halley, for whom simply being able to do their work effectively in a building that encourages not only efficiency but also well-being is enough. But this extraordinary-looking building, designed from first principles yet futuristic in appearance, whose visitors will probably never exceed a few hundred, has an impact that is being felt around the world – and possibly beyond.

Since completion the British Antarctic Survey has collaborated with the European Space Agency, NASA and the US National Science Foundation on ground-breaking experiments at Halley. The station has achieved Global Atmospheric Watch status and has become an icon for some of the most significant science being conducted on our planet today.

HALLEY VI Vital Statistics

KEY DATES

August 2004
Royal Institute of British Architects (RIBA) and Malcolm Reading Consultants launch competition for design of Halley VI

8 July 2005
Hugh Broughton Architects & Faber Maunsell (now AECOM) announced as competition winners

August 2005 – October 2007
Design and prefabrication phases

December 2007 – February 2012
On-site construction phase

28 February 2012
Halley VI is handed over to BAS

5 February 2013
Halley VI is officially launched in London

PERFORMANCE DATA

U value of cladding
0.113 W/m²K

Air infiltration rate
0.1 m³/h/m² at 50 Pa

Water usage
20 litres/person/day

Fuel saving
7% reduction/m² compared to Halley V

VITAL STATISTICS

Gross internal floor area
1510 m²

Blue modules
152 m²

Large red module
479 m²

Modules are raised around 4 metres above the ice level.

The skis measure 3.9 metres long and 1.1 metres wide

Halley VI comprises:

16 twin bedrooms
3 shared bathrooms
6 WCs

Quiet room at the north end of the station for people to contemplate the Antarctic environment in peace.
Communications and air traffic control centre
Station Leader's Office
Laundry
Doctor's surgery with operating capacity
Hairdressing cupboard
Computer server room
Two boot rooms
Dining room
Kitchen and food stores
Bar and games area
TV and internet lounge
Gym/music room
Workshops and plant rooms
Waste treatment and compaction rooms
Fuel storage
Science office
Laboratories
Science workshops
Science stores
Meteorological observatory

Separate buildings around the main station provide:

Garage
Summer and emergency accommodation
Balloon launching module
Clean air laboratory
Remote science modules linked to various radar arrays

FEATURES

Water is created using two melt tanks buried in the ice.

The sewage treatment is based on equipment made for ships and uses membrane bioreactor technology. This produces a combination of clean-water effluent (which is dropped back into the ice) and centrifugally dried sludge for incineration on site.

The base uses a vacuum drainage system.

The Base utilises combined heat and power (CHP) with heat captured off the generators to provide heating in the station so that only a small boiler is needed for top-up heating.

The modules are so well sealed and insulated that the majority of the heat load can be provided using the heat from the generators. On the occasions when additional heating is required, two boilers have been installed and operate as required by the BMS.

The station consumes 7 percent less fuel per m² than the previous station, Halley V. It delivers a significantly enhanced environment for living and working in Antarctica with far better controls to aid residents' comfort.

Ventilation systems incorporate plate heat exchangers to utilise the inherent warmth in extract air to heat the freezing fresh air intake. When cooling is required, the air is heated less.

HALLEY VI Suppliers

Access equipment	AJ Access Platforms (UK)
Access equipment ancillaries	Access Plant Sales (UK)
Acoustic enclosures	The Acoustic Enclosure Company (UK)
Acoustic steel door sets	IR Martin Roberts (UK)
Air handling equipment	Lindab (UK)
Air handling equipment	Trox Technik (UK)
Air handling equipment	Maine Engineering (UK)
Air handling equipment	Ruskin Air Management (UK)
Air traffic control desk	Thinking Space (UK)
Air transfer grilles	Lorient Polyproducts (UK)
Aluminium flashings	Metool Co (UK)
Analogue clocks	Wharton Electronics (UK)
Audio visual equipment	AVM Education(UK)
Bathroom fittings and ancillaries	Frank Sissons (UK)
Bathroom fittings and ancillaries	PTS (UK)
Brattberg ports	MCT Brattburg UK)
Bulkhead insulated panels	Eldapoint (UK)
Bunk bed units	Limelight Direct (UK)
Cable supplier	Eland cables (UK)
Cabooses	EIC (UK)
Carpets	Interface (UK)
Central module glazing system	Raico (Germany)
Cladding and steel frame	Antarctic Marine and Climate Centre (RSA)
Coffee tables	John Weaver (UK)
Control software and sensors	Schneider Electric (UK)
Curtains	Jo Hardy Furnishings (UK)
Curved double glazed cockpit rooflights	Oktatube (Netherlands)
Decorative materials	PPG Architectural Coatings (UK)
Dobson table and bearings	Felcon Limited (UK)
Dobson telescope fabrication works	Sondon Engineering (UK)
DOW silicone	ALSCO (UK)
Durat worktops	Solidity (UK)
Electric ancillaries	RS Components (UK)
Emergency evacuation equipment	HCL (UK)
Emergency evacuation equipment	Pammenter & Petrie (UK)
Feature aluminium ceiling lighting panel	Argent Fabrications (UK)
Feature aluminium ceiling panel and ceiling systems	Hunter Douglas (UK)
Fire extinguishers	Spectrum Safety (UK)
Fire protection equipment	SD Fire Alarms (UK)
Fire protection systems	ADT Fire & Security (UK)
Fixings	EJOT UK (UK)
Flag pole	Windsock Company (UK)
Flexible connectors between modules	Trelleborg (UK)
Floor access panels	Surespan (UK)
Floor finishes and ancillaries	T&R Flooring (UK)
Flooring tools and ancillaries	Sweeney Todd Blades (UK)
Fridge freezers	Griffiths & Nielsen (UK)
Furnishings	Coexistence (UK)
Furnishings	IKEA (UK)
Galvanised decking	Lionweld Kennedy Flooring (UK)
General building materials	E H Smith (UK)
General electrical materials	Edmundsons (UK)
General electrical materials	City Electrical Factors (UK)
General electrical materials	Newey & Eyre (UK)
General fabrication works	Twigg Fabrication (UK)
General fabrication works	Fredan Engineering (UK)
General fire proofing materials	Nullifire (UK)
General fire proofing materials and fixings	Hilti (UK)
General fixings and ancillaries	Fixings Direct (UK)
General hydraulic components	Advanced Hydraulics (UK)
General materials	Screwfix (UK)
General materials	Häfele (UK)
General materials	Build Center (UK)
General materials and PPE	Arco (UK)
General materials, small tools and equipment	Reynolds Group (South Africa)
General materials, small tools and equipment	Twigg (UK)
General plumbing materials	Wolseley (UK)
General plumbing materials	BSS (UK)
General timber merchant	Arnold Lavers (UK)
Generators	Westac Power (UK)
Glass shelving	Glass Shelf.co.uk (UK)
Glass shelving and splashbacks	Rugby Glass (UK)
GRP ceilings and window surrounds	Brecknell Willis Composites (UK)
GRP fabrication works	Millfield FRP (UK)
Gym and leisure equipment	Furniture File (UK)
Hydraulics	Titan (UK)
Incinerators	Todaysure (UK)
Insulated sewage pipe	Gill Insulations (UK)

Integrated fridges	W A Weston (UK)
Internal flame resistant coatings	Contego (USA)
Ironmongery	Yannedis (UK)
Jack assemblies	TEC Engineering (UK)
Joinery	Milner & Plant (UK)
Kitchen equipment and fittings	Intracat (UK)
Laboratory equipment	Wolf Laboratories (UK)
Laundry plinth	Crown Structural Engineering (UK)
LED bulkhead lighting	Gemma Lighting (UK)
M&E Traffolite labels	Identitag (UK)
Mantis crane	Scott Powerline & Utility Equipment (USA)
Mattresses, bedding and bunk curtains	RP Trading (UK)
Mechanical works ancillaies	Tapes Direct (UK)
Metal first aid cabinets	E A Broadburn (UK)
Movement joints	Movement Joints UK (UK)
Nanogel insulated glazing	Okalux (Germany)
Notice boards	Spaceright Europe (UK)
Office furnishings	Oracle Storage Systems (UK)
Office furnishings and equipment	Data Sound (UK)
Office safe	Insight (UK)
Partition walling products	Encon (UK)
Partition walling products	FGF (UK)
Permanent signage	QC Signs (UK)
Picador matting	Jaymart (UK)
Pipe insulation	Western Thermal (UK)
Plant room and general door sets, spiral staircase panels	Gatewood Joinery (UK)
Prefabricated joinery	Joyce and Reddington (UK)
Prefabricated M&E installations	Merit Merrell (UK)
Prefabricated rooms (bedrooms, bathrooms, office areas)	Servacomm (UK)
Prefabricated timber floor cassettes	Framework CDM (UK)
Recycling equipment	Orwak Environmental (UK)
Recycling equipment	Lesco Products (UK)
Recycling equipment	Home Recycling (UK)
Rollatore shelving	Railex Systems (UK)
Rubber floors	Freudenberg Norament (UK)
Sangenic units	Countrywide Healthcare (UK)
Scaffolding	SGB (UK)
Screen doors and graphics	Fendor (UK)

Service suspension systems	Gripple (UK)
Shelving	HC Slingsby (UK)
Site clothing	Pellacraft (UK)
Ski foundations	Lehmann (Germany)
Ski racks	Shopatron (UK)
Social module spiral staircase	Spiral Staircase Systems (UK)
Soft drinks dispenser equipment	Nichols Dispense (UK)
South Africa logistics	P&M Packing (South Africa)
South Africa logistics	Kwela Logisitcs (South Africa)
Speaker microphones	Tardis (UK)
Specialist plumbing	MRH Marine (UK)
Specialist lighting systems	Luxonic Lighting (UK)
Specialist sealants	Adshead Radcliffe (UK)
Specialist seals	Whitby & Chandler (UK)
Specialist timber floor beams	RTC Timber Systems (UK)
Sprinkler system	Marioff (UK)
Stainless steel splashbacks	Shine (UK)
Steps	Ladder Store (UK)
Storage cabinets	EDP Europe (UK)
Surgery equipment	Brandon Medical (UK)
Suspended ceiling systems	CCF (UK)
Temporary steelwork protection	Custom Covers (UK)
Threshold strips	Custom Audio Designs (UK)
Timber staircases	Specialist Woodworks (UK)
Tower fabrication	Swann Consulting (UK)
UK logistics	International Export Packers (UK)
Undercounter fridge	Currys (UK)
Vacuum drainage equipment	Gertsen & Olufsen (DK)
Vacuum drainage system	Blücher (UK)
Vacuum drainage system	Jets Group (Denmark)
Vynagrip matting	Plastic Extruders Limited (UK)
Wall access panels	Profab Access (UK)
Wall map case	Design Animations (UK)
Wall protection systems	SDS Protection (UK)
Washing machines and tumble dryers	Goodman Sparks (UK)
WC and shower cubicles	TBS Fabrications (UK)
Whiteboards	Ultralon (UK)
Window blinds	Luxaflex UK (UK)
Window blinds	P & M Blinds (UK)
Window seals	Silicone Altimex (UK)

CLIENT

British Antarctic Survey
www.antarctica.ac.uk

NERC
(Natural Environment
Research Council)
www.nerc.ac.uk

ARCHITECT

Hugh Broughton Architects
www.hbarchitects.co.uk

ENGINEERING DESIGN

AECOM
www.aecom.com

MAIN CONTRACTOR

Galliford Try International
www.gallifordtry.co.uk

SUBCONSULTANTS

HYDRAULIC LEG ENGINEERING
Bennett Associates

CLADDING CONSULTANTS
Billings Design Associates

COLOUR PSYCHOLOGIST
Colour Affects

AWARDS

The British Safety Council Awards 2011
International Safety Award

American Institute of Architects (AIA) UK
Excellence in Design Awards 2013
Winner

Royal Institute of British Architects (RIBA) Awards 2013
International Award for Architecture

British Construction Industry Awards (BCIA) 2013
International Project of the Year

The Structural Awards 2013
Sustainability Award

Civic Trust Award 2014
Civic Trust Awards
Special Award for Sustainability 2014

Engineering News-Record (ENR) 2014
Best Global Education/Research Project
Best Global Project 2014

Architizer A+ Awards 2014
Higher Education/Research Award
Art and Science Award

Institution of Civil Engineers (ICE) Engineering Awards 2014
Designed in London Award

Chicago Athenaeum International Architecture Award 2014
Winner

International Design Awards 2014
First Prize, Institutional

American Society of Civil Engineers (ASCE) Awards 2015
Award of Merit
Outstanding Civil Engineering Achievement (OCEA) Award